Published in the USA by
Chariot Victor Publishing
4050 Lee Vance View
Colorado Springs
CO 80918
USA

Copyright © 2000 John Hunt Publishing Ltd

Text © 2000 Mark Water

Illustrations © Bob Bond

Designed by
ANDREW MILNE DESIGN

All rights reserved. Except for brief quotations in critical articles or reviews, no part of this book may be reproduced in any manner without prior written permission from the publishers.

Faith Kids™ is a registered trademark of Cook Communications Ministries

ISBN 0-78143-317-7

Scriptures quoted from the International Children's Bible,
New Century Version (Anglicised Edition)
copyright © 1991 by Nelson Word Ltd, Milton Keynes, England.
Used by permission.

Write to: John Hunt Publishing Ltd
46A West Street, Alresford, Hampshire SO24 9AU, UK

The rights of Mark Water as author and Bob Bond as illustrator
of this work have been asserted in accordance with the
Copyright, Designs and Patents Act 1988.

Printed in Malaysia.

CONTENTS

pages 4-13
Mr. Noah Built an Ark

pages 14-23
Joseph: Prisoner to Vice President

pages 24-35
Moses and His Waterproof Cradle

pages 36-45
Teenager David versus Giant Goliath

pages 46-53
Daniel and the Day the Lions Did Not Eat

pages 54-61
Jonah and His Fishy Tale

page 62-64
Answers

OLD TESTAMENT ACTIVITY BIBLE

Mr. Noah Starts to Build

God said to Noah,
"Build a boat"
GENESIS 6: 13-14

Noah was a good man. He was the most innocent man of his time. He walked with God. Noah had three sons: Shem, Ham and Japheth.

People on earth did what God said was evil. Violence was everywhere. God saw this evil. All the people on earth did only evil. So God said to Noah, "People have made the earth full of violence. So I will destroy all people from the earth. Build a boat of cypress wood for yourself. Make rooms in it and cover it inside and outside with tar. This is

FACT FILE

a: How long was the boat?
b: How wide was the boat?
c: How high was the boat?
(Look up Genesis 6:15)

d: A modern plane like the Boeing 747 is about 230 feet long.. Was Noah's Ark longer or shorter than a modern plane?

BRAINTEASER

How many double decker buses could you have fitted into Noah's ark?

　　a: 3?
　　b: 24?
　　c: 432?

Mr. Noah Built an Ark

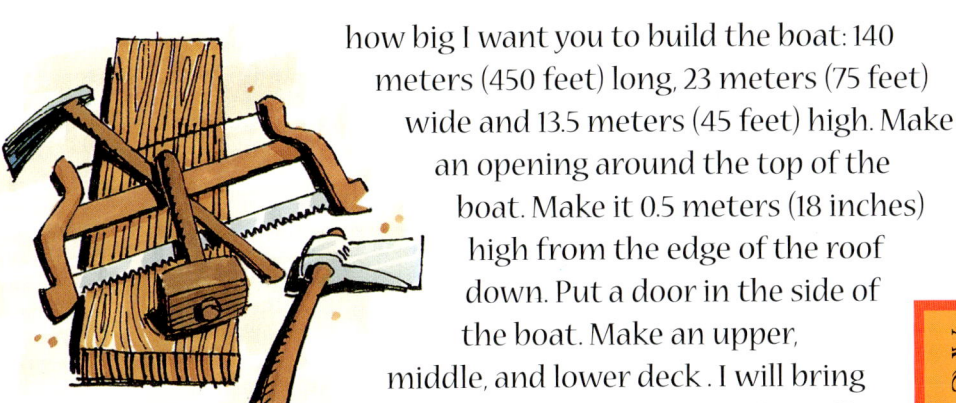

how big I want you to build the boat: 140 meters (450 feet) long, 23 meters (75 feet) wide and 13.5 meters (45 feet) high. Make an opening around the top of the boat. Make it 0.5 meters (18 inches) high from the edge of the roof down. Put a door in the side of the boat. Make an upper, middle, and lower deck. I will bring a flood of water on the earth. I will destroy all living things that live under the sky. This includes every-thing that has the breath of life.

Everything on the earth will die. But I will make an agreement with you. You, your sons, your wife, and your sons' wives will all go into the boat."

CHECK IT OUT!
GENESIS 6: 9-18

ACTIVITY TIME

From the letters below make up words. Five points for each word found linked to the story on these pages. One point for other words, up to a maximum of five words.

COVER IT WITH TAR INSIDE AND OUT

SPOT IN THE PICTURE

Five things which Noah needs to build his ark with.

IS THAT WHERE THE KITCHEN IS GOING TO BE?

OLD TESTAMENT ACTIVITY BIBLE

MR. NOAH COLLECTS THE ANIMALS

"There will be two of every kind of bird, animal and crawling thing."
GENESIS 6:20

God said to Noah, "Also, you must bring into the boat two of every living thing, male and female. Keep them alive with you. There will be two of every kind of bird, animal, and crawling thing. They will come to you to be kept alive. Also, gather some food. Store it on the boat as food for you and the animals."

Noah did everything that God commanded him.

MAKE A LIST
Write down the names of all the birds you can think of.

QUIZ
How did Noah please God?
Hint: Genesis 6:22

MRS. NOAH
Mrs. Noah is looking for the largest animals she can find. What are the names of the four she has found?

Mr. Noah Built an Ark

CHECK IT OUT!
GENESIS 6:19-22

WORD SEARCH

Make a list of the seven insects hidden in this word search. They are all written across or down.

A	N	T	Q	Y	Z	S
C	B	D	R	S	T	P
V	W	F	L	Y	Q	I
Q	W	E	R	T	Y	D
U	I	O	P	A	S	E
M	O	T	H	F	J	R
B	E	E	T	L	E	Z
L	Z	X	C	E	V	C
B	E	E	M	A	Q	Z

SPOT IN THE PICTURE

Mr. Noah has sent out his three sons to find food for the animals, birds, and insects, so he can store it all in the ark.

Find the three piles of fruit they made.

They hid them from the animals, but have forgotten where they put them!

7

OLD TESTAMENT ACTIVITY BIBLE

All Aboard the Ark

"Go into the ark, you and your whole family."
GENESIS 7:1

FIND THE MISSING...

Two pairs of striped animals are still hiding. Can you spot them? What are they called?

Then the Lord said to Noah, "I have seen that you are the best man among the people of this time. So you and your family go into the boat. Take with you seven pairs, each male with its female, of every kind of clean animal. And take one pair, each male with its female, of every kind of unclean

ACTIVITY TIME

From the letters below, see how many different words for animals, birds, insects, and reptiles you can find.

YOU ARE THE BEST MAN AMONG THE PEOPLE

FACT FILE

Clean means "animals fit for eating." Unclean means "animals that must not be eaten."

How many pairs of all the birds did Noah take?

Mr. Noah Built an Ark

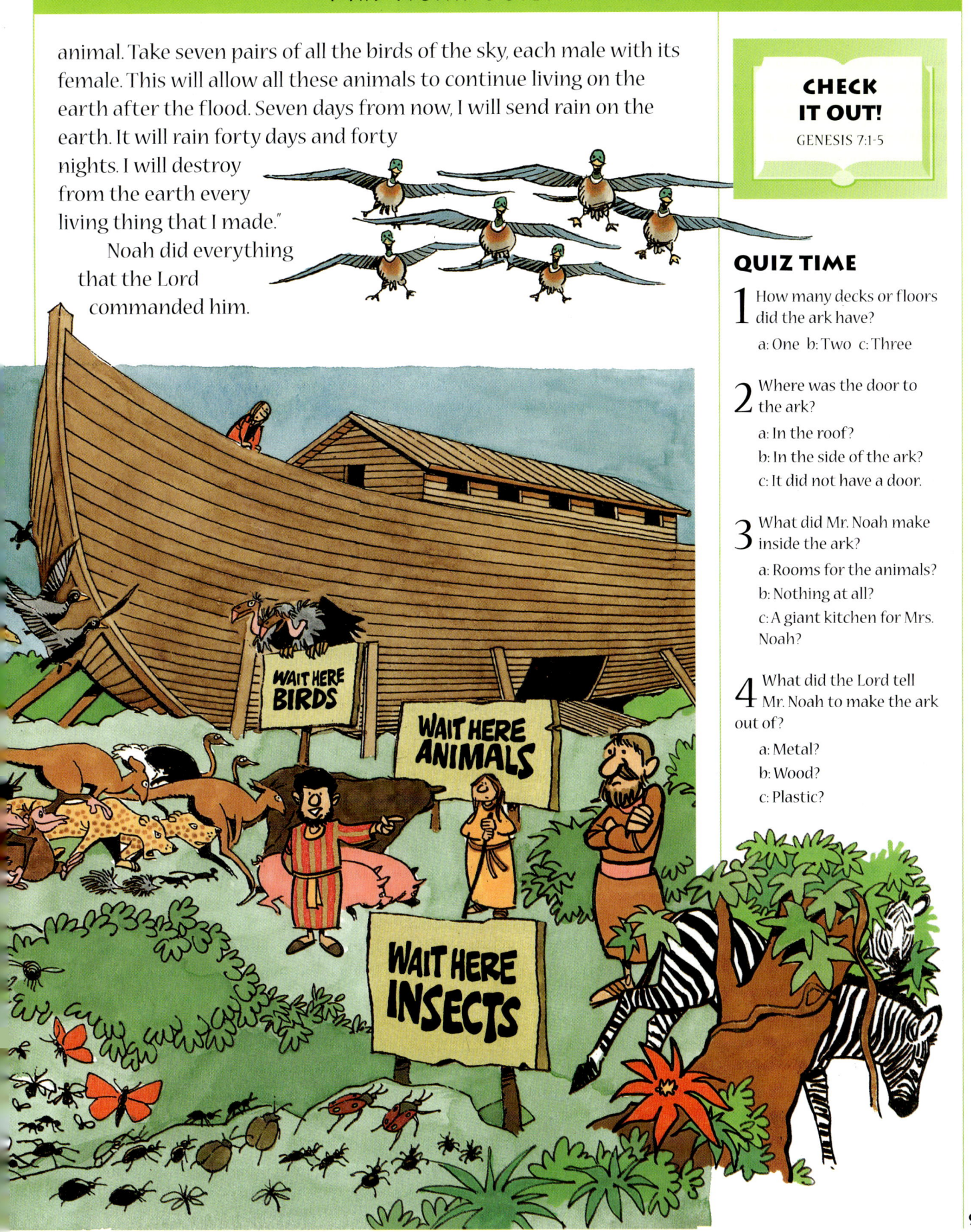

animal. Take seven pairs of all the birds of the sky, each male with its female. This will allow all these animals to continue living on the earth after the flood. Seven days from now, I will send rain on the earth. It will rain forty days and forty nights. I will destroy from the earth every living thing that I made."

Noah did everything that the Lord commanded him.

CHECK IT OUT!
GENESIS 7:1-5

QUIZ TIME

1 How many decks or floors did the ark have?
   a: One b: Two c: Three

2 Where was the door to the ark?
   a: In the roof?
   b: In the side of the ark?
   c: It did not have a door.

3 What did Mr. Noah make inside the ark?
   a: Rooms for the animals?
   b: Nothing at all?
   c: A giant kitchen for Mrs. Noah?

4 What did the Lord tell Mr. Noah to make the ark out of?
   a: Metal?
   b: Wood?
   c: Plastic?

OLD TESTAMENT ACTIVITY BIBLE

IT RAINS, AND RAINS, AND RAINS

And rain fell on the earth for forty days and forty nights.
GENESIS 7:12

ACTIVITY TIME

U-N-J-U-M-B-L-E

1. The names of Mr. Noah's three sons:
   a: Hems
   b: Mah
   c: Hehjapt

2. Mr. Noah's three sons took their seviw into the ark with them.

BRAINTEASER

Who am I?

My first is in shawl but not in wall.

My second is in blast and also in fast.

My third is in crummy as well as in yummy.

My whole tastes tasty in my tummy.

Hint: he went into the ark.

MR. NOAH BUILT AN ARK

Noah and his wife and his sons and their wives went into the boat to escape the waters of the flood. Seven days later the flood started.

The rain fell on the earth for forty days and forty nights.

On the same day Noah and his wife, his sons Shem, Ham and Japheth, and their wives went into the boat. They had every kind of wild animal and tame animal. There was every kind of animal that crawls on the earth. Every kind of bird was there. They all came to Noah in the boat in groups of two. There was every creature that had the breath of life. One male and one female of every living thing came. It was just as God had commanded Noah. Then the Lord closed the door behind them.

Water flooded the earth for forty days. As the water rose, it lifted the boat off the ground. The water continued to rise, and the boat floated on the water above the earth. The water rose so much that even the highest mountains under the sky were covered by it. The water continued to rise until it was more than twenty feet above the mountains.

And the waters continued to cover the earth for 150 days.

CHECK IT OUT!
GENESIS 7:7, 10, 12, 13-18, 20, 24

FIND THE MISSING...

Mrs. Noah is very upset! She has lost three things. Can you find her comb, her coat, and her belt?

FACT FILE

1 The flood water rose up the hills and mountains.

Did the water flood the earth so that the ark rose:

   a: Nearly as high as the tops of the mountains?
   b: The same height as the tops of the mountains?
   c: More than 20 feet (6.9 meters) higher than the tops of the mountains?

2 How many people went into the ark?

   a: 800 people
   b: 80 people
   c: 8 people

SPOT IN THE PICTURE

❖ Animals
❖ Birds
❖ Insects
❖ Reptiles

Old Testament Activity Bible

THE RAINBOW

"When the rainbow appears in the clouds, I will see it."
GENESIS 9:16

Then God said to Noah, "You and your wife, your sons and their wives should go out of the boat. Bring every animal out of the boat with you — the birds, animals and everything that crawls on the earth. Let them have many young ones and let them grow in number."

So Noah went out with his sons, his wife, and his sons' wives. Every animal, everything that crawls on the earth, and every bird went out of the boat. They left by families.

Then Noah built an altar to the Lord. The Lord was pleased with

DECODE

Use the code a=1, b=2, c=3, and so on, to decode the following message:

9 – 1 / 13 – 16 /
21 / 20 / 20 / 9 /
14 / 7 – 13 / 25 –
18 / 1 / 9 / 14 / 2 /
15 / 23 – 9 / 14 –
20 / 8 / 5 – 3 / 12 /
15 / 21 / 4 / 19

FACT FILE

The rainbow has seven colors in it.

a: What are the seven colors?
Hint: the first letters for each color are: B, G, I, O, R, V, Y.

b: Put the colors in the correct order.

c: Which color is at the top of the rainbow?

d: Which color is at the bottom of the rainbow?

MR. NOAH BUILT AN ARK

Noah's sacrifices. He said to himself, "I will never again curse the ground because of human beings... As long as the earth continues, there will be planting and harvest. Cold and hot, summer and winter, day and night will not stop."

Then God blessed Noah and his sons. He said to them, "Have many children. Grow in number and fill the earth. Every animal on earth and every bird in the sky will respect you. And God said, "I am making an agreement between Me and you and every living creature that is with you. It will continue from now on. This is the sign: I am putting my rainbow in the clouds.

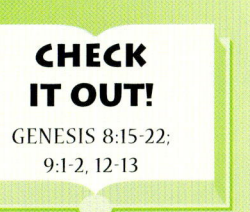

CHECK IT OUT!
GENESIS 8:15-22; 9:1-2, 12-13

DRAW YOUR OWN PICTURE

Draw a picture of this story, based on the picture on these pages.

Include Noah's ark, the rainbow, a bird, an animal, and something that crawls on the earth.

WORD SEARCH

Make a list of the six words hidden in this word search which come from the story on these pages. They are all written across, down and backwards.

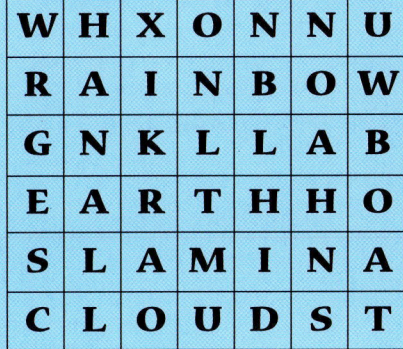

W	H	X	O	N	N	U
R	A	I	N	B	O	W
G	N	K	L	L	A	B
E	A	R	T	H	H	O
S	L	A	M	I	N	A
C	L	O	U	D	S	T

13

OLD TESTAMENT ACTIVITY BIBLE

Joseph's Special Robe

Jacob made Joseph a special robe with long sleeves.
GENESIS 37:3

Jacob lived in the land of Canaan, where his father had lived. When Joseph was seventeen years old, he and his brothers cared for the flocks. His brothers were the sons of Bilhah and Zilpah, his father's wives. Joseph gave his father bad reports about his

ACTIVITY TIME

Make up words from the letters below. Five points for each word found linked to the story on these pages. One point for other words, up to a maximum of five words.

THEY HATED THEIR BROTHER

QUIZ

1. How old was Joseph?

2. What did Joseph and his brothers do during the day?

3. Give one reason why Joseph was hated by his brothers?

4. Give a second reason why Joseph was hated by his brothers?

JOSEPH: PRISONER TO VICE PRESIDENT

brothers. Joseph was born when his father Israel, also called Jacob, was old. So Israel loved Joseph more than his other sons. He made Joseph a special robe with long sleeves. Joseph's brothers saw that their father loved Joseph more than he loved them. So they hated their brother and could not speak to him politely.

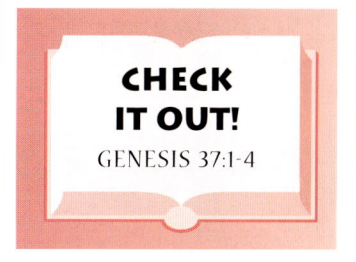

CHECK IT OUT!
GENESIS 37:1-4

BRAINTEASER
Find the message and write it out on a piece of paper.

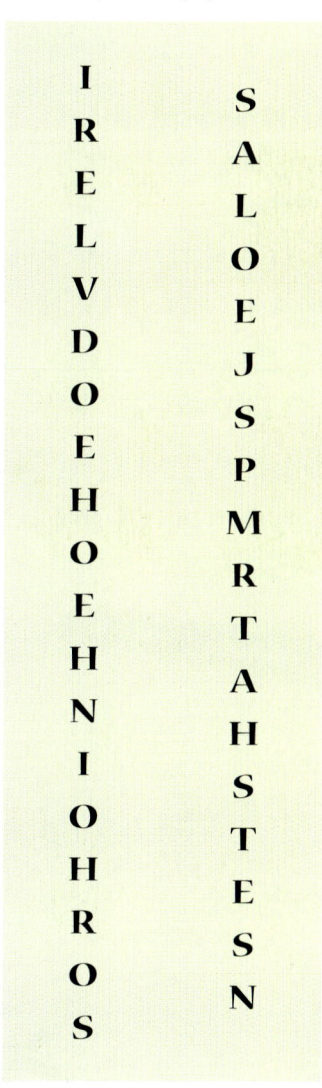

```
I          S
R          A
E          L
L          O
V          E
D          J
O          S
E          P
H          M
O          R
E          T
H          A
N          H
I          S
O          T
H          E
R          S
O          N
S
```

SPOT IN THE PICTURE
❖ Jacob
❖ Joseph's brothers.

15

Old Testament Activity Bible

Joseph the Dreamer

One night Joseph had a dream.
GENESIS 37:5

U-N-J-U-M-B-L-E

Write or, or say, in the correct order.

ELEVEN ME
SAW DOWN
I TO
BOWING
SUN THE
STARS AND
MOON

DRAW

Draw one of Joseph's dreams.

Then color or paint it.

SPOT IN THE PICTURE

❖ The sun
❖ The moon
❖ eleven stars

One night Joseph had a dream. When he told his brothers about it, they hated him even more. Joseph said, "Listen to the dream I had. We were in the field tying bundles of wheat together. My bundle stood up, and your bundles of wheat gathered around mine. Your bundles bowed down to mine."

His brothers said, "Do you really think you will be king over us? Do you truly think you will rule over us?" His brothers hated him even more now. They hated him because of his dreams and what he had said.

Then Joseph had another dream. He told his brothers about it also. He said, "Listen, I had another dream. I saw the sun, moon, and eleven stars bowing down to me."

Joseph also told his father about this dream. But his father scolded him saying, "What kind of dream is this? Do you really believe that your mother, your brothers, and I will bow down to you?" Joseph's brothers were jealous of him. But his father thought about what all these things could mean.

JOSEPH: PRISONER TO VICE PRESIDENT

CHECK IT OUT!
GENESIS 37:5-11

MATCH UP

Make five pairs from the ten objects.

a: eleven brothers

b: Joseph

c: the moon

d: eleven bundles of wheat, bowing

e: eleven brothers

f: the sun

g: Jacob

h: Joseph's mother

i: eleven stars, bowing

j: one bundle of wheat, not bowing

17

OLD TESTAMENT ACTIVITY BIBLE

Joseph Down a Well

They threw Joseph into the well.
GENESIS 37:24

Joseph's brothers saw him coming from far away. Before he reached them, they made a plan to kill him. They said to each other, "Here comes that dreamer. Let's kill him and throw his body into one of the wells. We can tell our father that a wild animal killed him. Then we will see what will become of his dreams."

CLOCKWORDS

In this puzzle there are two letters in place of each number on the clock face. To make a clockword, write down the letters of the hour hand mentioned, then the letters of the minute hand mentioned. So twenty to ten equals DU ST.

On a piece of paper fill in the blanks in the following sentence, using clockwords.

"Throw him _____ in the desert."
a: Two o'clock
b: Half past nine
c: Quarter past four
d: Five past eleven

JOSEPH: PRISONER TO VICE PRESIDENT

But Reuben heard their plan and saved Joseph. He said, "Let's not kill him. Don't spill any blood. Throw him into this well here in the desert. But don't hurt him!" Reuben planned to save Joseph later and send him back to his father. So when Joseph came to his brothers, they pulled off his robe with long sleeves and threw him into the well. It was empty. There was no water in it.

While Joseph was in the well, the brothers sat down to eat. When they looked up, they saw a group of Ishmaelites. They were traveling from Gilead to Egypt. Their camels were carrying spices, balm, and myrrh. The brothers took Joseph out of the well. They sold him to the Ishmaelites.

CHECK IT OUT!
GENESIS 37: 18-25, 28

UNSCRAMBLE
What were the three things the Ishmaelites had loaded on their camels?
a: iesspc
b: lamb
c: ymhrr

DECODE
Look at the symbols below each letter and then decode the six words in code to see why Reuben was a good brother.

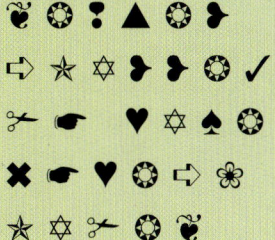

SPOT IN THE PICTURE
❖ The well
❖ Joseph's robe with long sleeves

Old Testament Activity Bible

Joseph as a Slave

Potiphar bought Joseph from the Ishmaelites.
GENESIS 39:1

Now Joseph had been taken down to Egypt. An Egyptian named Potiphar was an officer to the king of Egypt. He was the captain of the palace guard. He bought Joseph from the Ishmaelites who had brought him down there. The Lord was with Joseph, and he became a successful man. He lived in the house of his master, Potiphar the Egyptian.

Potiphar saw that the Lord was with Joseph... [and] made him

WORD SEARCH

Make a list of the six words hidden in this word search which come from the story on these pages. They are written across, down, up, and backwards.

A	B	H	A	P	P	Y	A
H	C	D	F	O	O	D	H
T	I	J	I	K	T	L	J
P	N	L	E	N	I	P	N
Y	Q	R	L	H	P	Z	B
G	S	T	D	U	H	T	H
E	U	V	W	X	A	X	G
A	T	N	A	V	R	E	S

20

JOSEPH: PRISONER TO VICE PRESIDENT

successful in everything he did. So Potiphar was very happy with Joseph. He allowed Joseph to be his personal servant and put him in charge of the house. Joseph was trusted with everything Potiphar owned... Then the Lord blessed the people in Potiphar's house because of Joseph. And the Lord blessed everything that belonged to Potiphar, both in the house and in the field... Potiphar was not concerned about anything, except the food he ate.

CHECK IT OUT!
GENESIS 39:1-6

QUIZ

1. What was Potiphar's job?
2. Who blessed the people in Potiphar's house?
3. Who did Potiphar buy Joseph from?

UNRAVEL

Potiphar knew the secret of Joseph's success.
What was it?

T X H X E X X L X
O X R X D X X W
X A X S X X W X I
X T X H X X J O X
S X E X P X H X

SPOT IN THE PICTURE

❖ Captain Potiphar
❖ Servant Joseph

OLD TESTAMENT ACTIVITY BIBLE

JOSEPH WELCOMES HIS FAMILY

Joseph kissed all his brothers.
GENESIS 45:15

ACTIVITY TIME

From the letters below, make up words. Five points for each word found linked to the story on these pages. One point for other words, up to a maximum of five words.

JOSEPH HUGGED HIS BROTHER BENJAMIN

RIGHT OR WRONG?

a: Plenty of food grew in the land of Canaan.

b: We will give them the best of what we have in Egypt.

SPOT IN THE PICTURE

- ❖ Joseph
- ❖ Six of his brothers
- ❖ Joseph's ring
- ❖ Joseph's fine linen clothes
- ❖ Joseph's gold chain

JOSEPH: PRISONER TO VICE PRESIDENT

The king said to Joseph, "Look! I have put you in charge of all the land of Egypt." Then the king took off his ring with the royal seal on it from his own finger and he put it on Joseph's finger. He gave Joseph fine linen clothes to wear. And he put a gold chain around Joseph's neck.

But no food grew in the land of Canaan. So the brothers hurried down to Egypt and stood before Joseph. Then Joseph hugged his brother Benjamin and cried. And Benjamin cried also. Then Joseph kissed all his brothers. He cried as he hugged them. After this, his brothers talked with him.

The king of Egypt and his officers learned that Joseph's brothers had come. And they were happy about this. So the king said to Joseph, "Tell your brothers to load their animals and go back to the land of Canaan and bring their father and their families back here to me. I will give them the best land in Egypt. And they will eat the best food we have here. Tell them to take some wagons from Egypt for their children and their wives…"

"Tell them not to worry about bringing any of their things with them. We will give them the best of what we have in Egypt."

CHECK IT OUT!
GENESIS 41:41-42; 43:1, 15; 45:14-20

SPOT THE WRONG THINGS

What are the four wrong things in each of the following two sentences?

a: The queen gave Joseph an earring, a pair of jeans and a silver chain.

b: Take some cars from America for their elephants and their donkeys.

BRAINTEASER

Change one letter in each of these words to make six words which appear in the story on these pages.

XGYPT

HPGGED

BEJJAMIN

QAGONS

FALILIES

YANAAN

Moses and His Waterproof Cradle

She put the baby in the basket.
EXODUS 2:3

QUIZ TIME

1. How many months was baby Moses hidden for?
2. What was baby Moses' basket made of?
3. What was used to make sure that baby Moses' basket floated in water?
4. What was the name of the river that baby Moses' basket was put in?

FACT FILE

THE RIVER NILE

1. The River Nile is:
   a: the shortest river in Egypt?
   b: the longest river in Egypt?

2. The River Nile is:
   a: 41 miles long (66 km)?
   b: 415 miles long (667 km)?
   c: 4150 miles long (6677 km)?

3. The River Nile is the longest river in the world.
   a: True?
   b: False?

The king commanded all his people: "Every time a boy is born to the Hebrews, you must throw him into the Nile River. But let all the girl babies live."

There was a man from the family of Levi. He married a woman who was also from the family of Levi. She became pregnant and gave birth to a son. She saw how wonderful the baby was, and hid him for three months. But after three months, she was not able to hide the baby any longer. So she got a basket made of reeds and covered it with tar so that it would float. She put the baby in the basket. Then she put the basket among the tall grass at the edge of the Nile River.

MOSES AND HIS WATERPROOF CRADLE

CHECK IT OUT!
EXODUS 1:22; 2:1-3

ACTIVITY TIME

Make a model basket and put a tiny model baby in it. See if you can make one that will float in water.

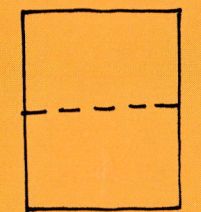

1. Take a piece of rectangular paper and fold in half across the width.

2. With the fold at the bottom, fold up the two bottom corners

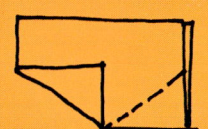

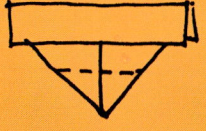

3. Fold over the remaining top pieces down each side. Fold up the point and tuck in.

4. Open out the cradle and tuck the top pieces into each other at the front and back.

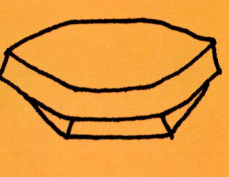

SPOT IN THE PICTURE

- The baby Moses
- His waterproof cradle
- The River Nile
- Tall grass

Old Testament Activity Bible

The Princess Finds Baby Moses

"This is one of the Hebrew babies."
EXODUS 2:6

The baby's sister stood a short distance away. She wanted to see what would happen to Moses.

Then the daughter of the king of Egypt came to the river to take a bath. Her servant girls were walking beside the river. She saw the basket in the tall grass. So she sent her slave girl to get it. The king's daughter opened the basket and saw the baby boy. He was crying, and she felt sorry for him. She said, "This is one of the Hebrew babies."

WORD SEARCH

Find six words about babies hidden in this word search. They are all written across or down.

M	I	L	K	A	X	R
O	B	F	H	J	Z	A
M	L	C	R	I	B	T
M	S	M	I	L	E	T
Y	C	M	K	D	Q	L
D	A	D	D	Y	L	E

THE KIND PRINCESS

What did the kind princess:
  a: see?
  b: feel?
  c: say?

MOSES AND HIS WATERPROOF CRADLE

Then the baby's sister asked the king's daughter, "Would you like me to find a Hebrew woman to nurse the baby for you?"

The king's daughter said, "Yes, please." So the girl went and got the baby's own mother.

The king's daughter said to the woman, "Take this baby and nurse him for me. I will pay you." So the woman took her baby and nursed him. After the child had grown older, the woman took him to the king's daughter. She adopted the baby as her own son. The king's daughter named him Moses, because she had pulled him out of the water.

CHECK IT OUT!
EXODUS 2:4-10

BRAINTEASER

Why did the kind princess go to the river:
   a: to have a bath?
   b: to row a boat?
   c: to paint a picture?

SPOT IN THE PICTURE

There are five women in the picture. Can you spot:
- the princess?
- a servant of the princess?
- Moses' sister?
- Moses' mother?

OLD TESTAMENT ACTIVITY BIBLE

MOSES ON THE RUN

Moses ran away from the king.
EXODUS 2:15

DECODE

Look at the symbols below each letter and then decode the six words in code

A	B	C	D	E	F	G	H	I
✡	▲	✜	✓	✷	✱	◆	❀	✏

J	K	L	M	N	O	P	Q	R
✖	⚲	★	◆	♣	☚	➪	✱	♥

S	T	U	V	W	X	Y	Z
♥	✂	❗	♠	◇	❕	✸	✠

✂ ❀ ✷

⚲ ✏ ♣ ◆

✂ ♥ ✏ ✷ ✓

✂ ☚

⚲ ✏ ★ ★

✜ ☚ ♥ ✷ ♥

28

MOSES AND HIS WATERPROOF CRADLE

Moses grew and became a man. One day he visited his people, the Hebrews. He saw that they were forced to work very hard. He saw an Egyptian beating a Hebrew man, one of Moses' own people. Moses looked all around and saw that no one was watching. So he killed the Egyptian and hid his body in the sand.

The next day, Moses returned and saw two Hebrew men fighting each other. He saw that one man was in the wrong. Moses said to that man, "Why are you hitting one of your own people?"

The man answered, "Who made you our ruler and judge? Are you going to kill me as you killed the Egyptian?"

Then Moses was afraid. He thought, "Now everyone knows what I did."

When the king heard about what Moses had done, he tried to kill Moses. But Moses ran away from the king and went to live in the land of Midian. There he sat down near a well.

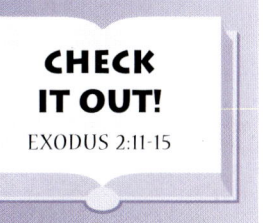

CHECK IT OUT!
EXODUS 2:11-15

FACT FILE
How far away was Midian from Egypt, where Moses ran away to?
- a: One mile?
- b: Between one and ten miles?
- c: Over a hundred miles?

QUIZ

1. When Moses reached Midian did he:
   - a: sit under a tree?
   - b: sit near a skyscraper?
   - c: sit near a well?

2. Moses killed a man for beating another man. Was the man Moses killed:
   - a: an Egyptian?
   - b: a Hebrew?

3. Moses was brought up as a prince in an Egyptian palace. Was he:
   - a: a Hebrew?
   - b: an Egyptian?

OLD TESTAMENT ACTIVITY BIBLE

Moses and the Amazing Bush

One day Moses was taking care of Jethro's sheep. Jethro was the priest of Midian and also Moses' father-in-law... Moses came to Sinai, the mountain of God. There the angel of the Lord appeared to Moses in flames of fire coming out of a bush. Moses saw that the bush was on fire, but it was not burning up. So Moses said, "I will go closer to this strange thing. How can a bush continue burning without burning up?"

The Lord saw Moses was coming to look at the bush. So God called to him from the bush, "Moses, Moses!"

Moses saw that the bush was on fire, but it was not burning up.
EXODUS 3:2

BRAINTEASER

From the last paragraph of the story on these pages:
- a: What had God heard?
- b: What had God seen?
- c: What was God concerned about?
- d: What was God about to do?

On a piece of paper write out the following sentence and color in the letters.

"I HAVE SEEN THE TROUBLES OF MY PEOPLE."

MOSES AND HIS WATERPROOF CRADLE

And Moses said, "Here I am."

Then God said, "Do not come any closer. Take off your sandals. You are standing on holy ground. I am the God of your ancestors. I am the God of Abraham, the God of Isaac, and the God of Jacob." Moses covered his face because he was afraid to look at God.

The Lord said, "I have seen the troubles my people have suffered in Egypt. And I have heard their cries when the Egyptian slave masters hurt them. I am concerned about their pain. I have come down to save them from the Egyptians. I will bring them out of that land. I will lead them to a good land with lots of room."

CHECK IT OUT!
EXODUS 3:1-8

QUIZ TIME
What was special about the new land God promised Moses:
- a: It had lots of room?
- b: It had fast cars?
- c: Everyone played baseball?
- d: There was much food?
- e: It was great for skiing?
- f: Every garden had a swing?

Two of the above six ideas are correct.

BACK TO FRONT
On a piece of paper write out these words in the correct order, or say them aloud in the correct order.

GROWS FOOD MUCH WHERE LAND A

Old Testament Activity Bible

Moses Leaves Egypt

"Go and worship the Lord."
EXODUS 12:31

During the night, the king called for Moses and Aaron. He said to them, "Get up and leave my people. You and your people may do as you have asked. Go and worship the Lord. Take all your sheep and cattle... Go. And also bless me." The Egyptians also asked the Israelites to hurry and leave. They said, "If you don't leave, we shall all die!"

The people of Israel took their dough before the yeast was added. They wrapped the bowls for making dough in clothing and carried them on their shoulders. The people of Israel did what Moses told them to do. They asked their Egyptian neighbors for things made of silver and gold and for clothing. The Lord caused the Egyptians to think well of the Israelites. So the Israelites took rich gifts from the Egyptians.

The Israelites traveled from Rameses to Succoth. There were about 600,000 men walking. This does not include the women and children. Many other people who were not Israelites went with them. A large number of sheep, goats and cattle went with them. The people of Israel had lived in Egypt for 430 years. That night the Lord kept watch to bring them out of Egypt. So on this same night the Israelites are to keep watch today. They are to do this to honor the Lord from now on.

ACTIVITY TIME

REACH FOR YOUR CALCULATOR

600,000 Israelite men left Egypt. If there were the same number of women and if there were twice as many children,

1 How many Israelite men, women and children left Egypt?

If there were twice as many sheep as there were children, if there were twice as many cattle as there were men, if there were half as many goats as there were women,

2 How many animals left Egypt?

3 In total, how many men, women, children, sheep, cattle and goats left Egypt?

Double points if you do this without a calculator!

SPOT IN THE PICTURE

- ❖ Clothes
- ❖ Goats
- ❖ Sheep
- ❖ Cattle

MOSES AND HIS WATERPROOF CRADLE

CHECK IT OUT!
EXODUS 12:31-38, 40, 42

ACTIVITY TIME

Bake or buy some unleavened bread (bread made without yeast).

Then, eat some of this unleavened bread with your next meal.

FIND THE MESSAGE

Write out the king's message to Moses. (Ignore the letters "X".)

"XGXEXTXX
UXPXXAXN
XDXXLXEXA
XVXEXXMX
YXXPXEXOX
PXLXEX."

BRAINTEASER

How long had God's people been slaves in Egypt for?
 a: 3 years?
 b: 43 years?
 c: 430 years?

OLD TESTAMENT ACTIVITY BIBLE

Moses Crosses Through the Red Sea

The Israelites went through the sea on dry land.
EXODUS 14:22

The Israelites saw the king and his army coming after them. They were very frightened and cried to the Lord for help. Moses answered, "Don't be afraid! Stand still and see the Lord save you today. You will never see these Egyptians again after today. You will only need to remain calm. The Lord will fight for you."

ACTIVITY TIME

Make a bookmark, using the following words:

The Lord will fight for you.
EXODUS 14:14

MOSES AND HIS WATERPROOF CRADLE

Then the Lord said to Moses, "Why are you crying out to me? Command the people of Israel to start moving. Raise your staff and hold it over the sea. The sea will split. Then the people can cross the sea on dry land."

Moses held his hand over the sea. All that night the Lord drove back the sea with a strong east wind. And so He made the sea become dry land. The water was split. And the Israelites went through the sea on dry land. A wall of water was on both sides.

CHECK IT OUT!
EXODUS 14:10, 13-16, 21-22

BRAINTEASER
Choose the correct sentence from each pair.

1. a: The Lord drove back the sea with a west wind.
b: The Lord drove back the sea with an east wind.

2. a: The Lord drove back the sea with a gentle wind.
b: The Lord drove back the sea with a strong wind.

3. a: The people crossed the sea in boats.
b: The people crossed the sea on dry land.

QUIZ TIME
Moses showed his faith in God in many ways.

1. What did God tell Moses to do with his staff?

2. What did God tell Moses to do with his hand?

OLD TESTAMENT ACTIVITY BIBLE

GOLIATH, THE CHAMPION

The Philistines had a champion fighter named Goliath.
1 SAMUEL 17:4

The Philistines had a champion fighter named Goliath. He was from Gath. He was nearly ten feet tall. He came out of the Philistine camp. He had a bronze helmet on his head, and he wore a coat of scale armor. It was made of bronze and weighed about 125 pounds. He wore bronze protectors on his legs and he had a small spear of bronze tied on his back. The wooden part of his larger spear was like a weaver's rod. And its blade weighed about 15 pounds. The officer who carried his shield walked in front of him.

Goliath stood and shouted to the Israelite soldiers, "Why have you taken positions for battle? I am a Philistine, and you are Saul's servants! Choose a man and send him to fight me. If he can fight and kill me, we will become your servants. But if I defeat and kill him, you will become our servants." Then he said, "Today I stand and dare the army of Israel! Send one of your men to fight me!" When Saul and the Israelites heard the Philistine's words, they were very afraid.

ACTIVITY TIME

Weigh yourself.
Work out how many times heavier Goliath's scale armor was than your weight.

BRAINTEASER

Change one letter of each of these words to make six words which appear in the story on these pages.

QRONZE
FIIHTER
AFVAID
PAUL
SPETR
HELMEY

Teenager David Versus Giant Goliath

CHECK IT OUT!
1 SAMUEL 17:4-11

SPOT IN THE PICTURE

- Goliath
- Goliath's helmet
- Goliath's coat of armor
- Goliath's small spear
- Goliath's larger spear

FIND THE MESSAGE

Write out Goliath's challenge to God's people.

"XTXOXDAX
YXXIXXSXT
XAXNXDXX
AXNXDXXD
XAXRXEXXT
XHXEXXAX
RXMXYXXO
XFXXIXSXR
XAXEXLX!X"
X

OLD TESTAMENT ACTIVITY BIBLE

DAVID BRINGS FOOD

"Take ten loaves of bread."
1 SAMUEL 17:17

Now Jesse said to his son David, "Take this forty-four pounds of cooked grain and ten loaves of bread. Take them to your brothers in the camp. Also take ten pieces of cheese. Give them to the commander of your brothers' group of 1,000 soldiers. See how your brothers are. Bring back something to show me they are all

QUIZ

1. What was the name of David's father?
2. Who was David told to take ten cheeses to?
3. What time of day did David leave home?

SPOT IN THE PICTURE

- The Philistine army
- The Israelite army
- David
- Cheese
- Bread

TEENAGER DAVID VERSUS GIANT GOLIATH

right. Your brothers are with Saul and the army in the Valley of Elah. They are fighting against the Philistines."

Early in the morning David left the sheep with another shepherd. He took the food and left as Jesse had told him.

When David arrived at the camp, the army was leaving. They were going out to their battle positions. The soldiers were shouting their war cry. The Israelites and Philistines were lining up their men to face each other in battle.

CHECK IT OUT!
1 SAMUEL 17:17-21

CLOCKWORDS

In this puzzle there are two letters in place of each number on the clock face. To make a clockword, write down the letters of the hour hand mentioned, then the letters of the minute hand mentioned. So twenty to ten equals MU ST.

On a piece of paper fill in the blanks in the following sentence, using clockwords.

a: Three o'clock
b: Half past two
c: Twenty past one
d: Five to nine
e: Twenty five past seven

---- brothers are ---- ---- and the ---- in the Valley of ----

OLD TESTAMENT ACTIVITY BIBLE

David Speaks Up

David left the food with the man who kept the supplies. Then he ran to the battle line and talked to his brothers. While he was talking with them, Goliath came out. He was the Philistine champion from Gath. He shouted things against Israel as usual, and David heard it. When the Israelites saw Goliath,

David said, "Why does Goliath think he can speak against the armies of the living God?"
1 SAMUEL 17:26

ACTIVITY TIME

From the letters below make up words. Five points for each word found linked to the story on these pages. One point for other words, up to a maximum of five words.

THEY SAID, "LOOK AT THIS MAN GOLIATH"

U-N-J-U-M-B-L-E

KING GOLIATH KILLS THE THE TO MAN MUCH GIVE WILL MONEY WHO.

Teenager David Versus Giant Goliath

they were very much afraid and ran away.

They said, "Look at this man Goliath. He keeps coming out to speak against Israel. The king will give much money to the man who kills Goliath. He will also give his daughter in marriage to whomever kills him. And his father's family will not have to pay taxes in Israel."

David asked the men who stood near him, "What will be done to reward the man who kills this Philistine? What will be done for whoever takes away the shame from Israel? Goliath is a Philistine. He is not circumcised. Why does he think he can speak against the armies of the living God?"

CHECK IT OUT!
1 SAMUEL 17: 22-26

BRAINTEASER

Find the message, and write it out on a piece of paper.

W E T E S A L T S A G L A H H

H N H I R E I E S W O I T T

Y E E Y U H F A D N R N W Y

E W R V R M C A R I A D A A A

SPOT IN THE PICTURE

❖ Goliath
❖ David
❖ The Israelite army

41

Old Testament Activity Bible

David Will Fight

Some men heard what David said and told Saul. Then Saul ordered David to be sent to him. David said to Saul, "Don't let anyone be discouraged. I, your servant, will go and fight this Philistine!"

Saul answered, "You can't go out against this Philistine and fight him. You're only a boy. Goliath has been a warrior since he was a young man."

But David said to Saul, "I, your servant, have been keeping my father's sheep. When a lion or bear came and took a sheep from the flock, I would chase it. I would attack it and save the sheep from its mouth. When it attacked me, I caught it by its fur. I would kill it. I, your servant, have killed both a lion and a bear! Goliath, the Philistine who is not circumcised, will be like the lion or bear I killed. He will die because he has stood against the armies of the living God. The Lord saved me from a lion and a bear. He will also save me from this Philistine."

David said, "I, your servant, will go and fight this Philistine!"
1 SAMUEL 17:32

DECODE

Look at the symbols below each letter and then decode the eighteen words in code

TEENAGER DAVID VERSUS GIANT GOLIATH

CHECK IT OUT!
1 SAMUEL 17:31-37

DRAW

Draw a picture of David looking after his sheep. Make sure you remember to put in a bear and a lion.

TRUE OR FALSE?

a: David was over thirty years old.
b: David was a shepherd.
c: Goliath had been a soldier since he was a young man.
d: Goliath was an Israelite.

SPOT IN THE PICTURE

- David
- Saul
- Saul's tent

43

OLD TESTAMENT ACTIVITY BIBLE

David's Victory

David took his stick in his hand, and he chose five smooth stones from a stream. He put them in his pouch and held his sling in his hand. Then he went to meet Goliath.

At the same time, the Philistine was coming closer to David. The man who held his shield walked in front of him. Goliath looked at David. He saw that David was only a boy, tanned and handsome. He looked down at David with disgust. He said, "Do you think I am a dog, that you come at me with a stick?" He used his gods' names to curse David. He said to David, "Come here. I'll feed your body to the birds of the air and the wild animals!"

But David said to him, "You come to me using a sword, a large spear, and a small spear. But I come to you in the name of the Lord of heaven's armies. He's the God of the armies of Israel!

David defeated the Philistine with only a sling and a stone!
1 SAMUEL 17:50

ACTIVITY TIME

Make a bookmark out of the following words.

The Lord does not need swords or spears to save people
1 SAMUEL 17: 47

Teenager David Versus Giant Goliath

You have spoken out against Him. Today the Lord will give you to me. I'll kill you, and I'll cut off your head. Today I'll feed the bodies of the Philistine soldiers to the birds of the air and the wild animals. Then all the world will know there is a God in Israel! Everyone gathered here will know the Lord does not need swords or spears to save people. The battle belongs to Him! And He will help us defeat all of you."

As Goliath came near to attack him, David ran quickly to meet him. He took a stone from his pouch. He put it into his sling and slung it. The stone hit the Philistine on his forehead and sank into it. Goliath fell face down on the ground.

So David defeated the Philistine with only a sling and a stone! He hit him and killed him. He fell to the ground and David cut off his head.

CHECK IT OUT!
1 SAMUEL 17:40-50

BACK TO FRONT
Write out, or say, in the correct order.

"! ISRAEL IN GOD A IS THERE KNOW WILL WORLD THE ALL THEN"

SPOT IN THE PICTURE
- Goliath
- David
- David's sling
- David's stone

BRAINTEASER
Find the six mistakes.

He took a dart from his pouch. He put it into his sling and slung it. The dart hit the Israelite on his nose and sank into it. Goliath fell backwards into the river.

OLD TESTAMENT ACTIVITY BIBLE

Daniel, the Good Citizen

Daniel was trustworthy.
DANIEL 6:4

Darius thought it would be a good idea to choose 120 governors. They would rule through all of his kingdom. And he chose three men as supervisors over those 120 governors. Daniel was one of those supervisors. The king set up these men so that he would not be cheated.

BRAINTEASER

Take out all the X letters and see why the governors did not like Daniel.

T X H X E X Y X /
X C X O X U X L X
D X / X N X O X T
X / X A X C X C X
U X S X E X / X H
X I X M X / X O X
F X / X D X O X I X
N X G X / X A X N
X Y X T X H X I X
N X G X / X W X R
X O X N X G X .

TRUE OR FALSE?

a: Daniel was rather lazy.
b: Daniel never cheated the king.
c: The supervisors found that Daniel did many bad things.
d: The king planned to put Daniel in charge of his whole kingdom.
e: Daniel did the best work out of all the supervisors and governors.

DANIEL AND THE DAY THE LIONS DID NOT EAT

Daniel showed that he could do the work better than the other supervisors and the governors. Because of this, the king planned to put Daniel in charge of the whole kingdom. So the other supervisors and the governors tried to find reasons to accuse Daniel. But he went on doing the business of the government. They could not find anything wrong with him, so they could not accuse him of doing anything wrong. Daniel was trustworthy. He was not lazy and did not cheat the king.

Finally these men said, "We will never find any reason to accuse Daniel. But we must find something to complain about. It will have to be about the law of his God."

CHECK IT OUT!
DANIEL 6:1-5

MATCH UP
Match up the pictures with the correct numbers.

1 2 0 — King

1 — Supervisor

3 — Governor

SPOT IN THE PICTURE
- Daniel
- Daniel's home
- Daniel's room
- A governor

Old Testament Activity Bible

Daniel Continues to Pray

Daniel prayed as he always had done.
DANIEL 6:10

SPOT IN THE PICTURE

- Daniel's room
- Daniel
- Anyone spying on Daniel

WORD SEARCH

Make a list of the six words hidden in this word search which come from the story on these pages. They are all written across or down.

M	K	N	E	E	S	S
W	I	N	D	O	W	S
N	N	P	E	V	S	T
V	G	R	N	P	K	Z
P	D	A	N	I	E	L
E	H	Y	Z	X	Q	I
J	E	T	Y	L	E	Z

So the supervisors and the governors went as a group to the king. They said: "King Darius, live forever! The supervisors, assistant governors, governors, the people who advise you and the captains of the soldiers have all agreed on something. We think the king should make this law that everyone would have to obey: no one should pray to any god or man except to you, our king. This should be done for the next thirty days. Anyone who doesn't obey will be thrown into the lions' den. Now, our king, make the law. Write it down so it cannot be changed. The laws of the Medes and Persians cannot be canceled." So King Darius made the law and had it written.

When Daniel heard that the new law had been written, he went to his house. He went to his upstairs room. The windows of that room opened towards Jerusalem. Three times each day Daniel got down on his knees and prayed. He prayed and thanked God, just as he always had done.

Then those men went as a group and found Daniel. They saw him praying and asking God for help.

The Law of the Medes

DANIEL AND THE DAY THE LIONS DID NOT EAT

CHECK IT OUT!
DANIEL 6:6-11

QUIZ

1. List four groups of people who were said to be in agreement.

2. Towards which town did Daniel pray?

3. For how many days would the new law last?

READ THE MESSAGE

Find out what would happen to anyone who disobeyed the new law.

X A X N X Y X O
X N X E X X W X
H X O X X D X O
X E X S X N X ' X
T X X O X B X E X
Y X X W X I X L X
L X X B X E X X T
X H X R X O X W
X N X X I X N X T
X O X X T X H X E
X X L X I X O X N
X S X ' X X X D X
E X N X .

49

OLD TESTAMENT ACTIVITY BIBLE

Daniel with the Lions

They threw Daniel into the lions' den.
DANIEL 6:16

So those men went to the king. They talked to him about the law he had made... Then they said, "Daniel is one of the captives from Judah. And he is not paying attention to the law you wrote. Daniel still prays to his God three times every day."

The king became very upset when he heard this. He decided he had to save Daniel. He worked until sunset trying to

DECODE

What message about Daniel was told to the king?

Look at the symbols below each letter and then decode the ten words in code:

A	B	C	D	E	F	G	H	I
✡	▲	✦	✓	✺	✳	♦	❀	✏

J	K	L	M	N	O	P	Q	R
✗	∞	★	❖	♘	☞	➪	✱	☘

S	T	U	V	W	X	Y	Z
♥	✂	❕	♠	◆	❴	✴	✠

SPOT IN THE PICTURE

- ❖ Daniel
- ❖ Lions
- ❖ Bones

DANIEL AND THE DAY THE LIONS DID NOT EAT

think of a way to save him.

Then those men went as a group to the king. They said, "Remember, our king, the law of the Medes and Persians. It says that no law or command given by the king can be changed."

So King Darius gave the order. They brought Daniel and threw him into the lions' den. The king said to Daniel, "May the God you serve all the time save you!" A big stone was brought. It was put over the opening of the lions' den. Then the king used his signet ring to put his special seal on the rock. And he used the rings of his royal officers to put their seals on the rock also. This showed that no one could move that rock and bring Daniel out.

CHECK IT OUT!
DANIEL 6:12-17

BRAINTEASER

What was the king's wish for Daniel? Follow the arrows to complete the sentence. Write it out on a piece of paper.

```
    M Y H G D O
U                O
Y                E
V                A
S                E
V                R
E                S
    A T E O Y U
```

SPOT THE MISTAKES

There are ten mistakes to find.

The queen became very upset when she saw this. She decided she had to punish David. She worked until sunrise trying to think of a way to punish him.

OLD TESTAMENT ACTIVITY BIBLE

DANIEL IS KEPT SAFE

"My God sent his angel to close the lions' mouths."
DANIEL 6:22

BRAINTEASER

Discover the last part of King Darius' letter.

Remove the letters
J K Z X U C B

J K G B O C X D J
B S C A U X V Z E
K D J - J K D X A
Z N U I C E L B
B F C R C O U M -
X T X H Z E Z
K P K O J W J E X
R Z - K O Z Z F J
B T J H K E K
J L X I B O C N Z
S J .

TRUE OR FALSE?

a: Daniel had his right hand bitten by a lion.

b: King Darius had hoped that Daniel would be gobbled up.

c: King Darius wrote a letter to support Daniel's God.

The next morning King Darius got up at dawn. He hurried to the lions' den. As he came near the den, he was worried. He called out to Daniel. He said, "Daniel, servant of the living God! Has your God that you always worship been able to save you from the lions?"

Daniel answered, "My king, live forever! My God sent His angel to close the lions' mouths. They have not hurt me, because my God knows that I am innocent. I never did anything wrong to you, my king."

King Darius was very happy. He told his servants to lift Daniel out of the lions' den. So they lifted him out and did not find any injury on him. This was because Daniel had trusted in his God.

Then King Darius wrote a letter. It was to all people and all nations...

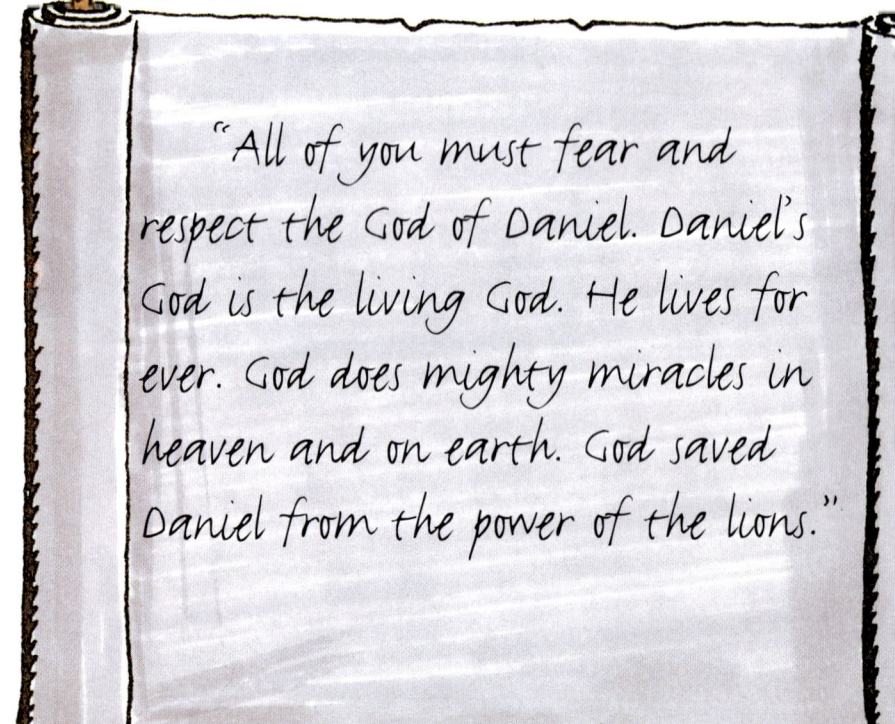

"All of you must fear and respect the God of Daniel. Daniel's God is the living God. He lives for ever. God does mighty miracles in heaven and on earth. God saved Daniel from the power of the lions."

DANIEL AND THE DAY THE LIONS DID NOT EAT

CHECK IT OUT!
DANIEL 6: 19-23, 25-27

ACTIVITY TIME

BOOKMARK

Make a bookmark, using the following words.

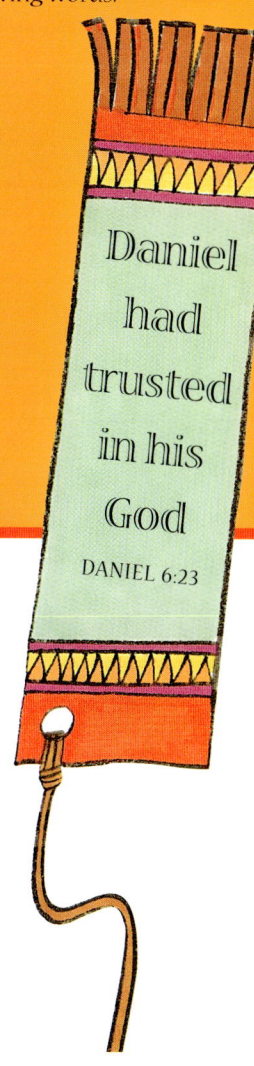

Daniel had trusted in his God
DANIEL 6:23

SPOT IN THE PICTURE
- Daniel
- Lions
- King Darius

OLD TESTAMENT ACTIVITY BIBLE

JONAH RUNS AWAY

Jonah got up to run away from the Lord.
JONAH 1:3

The Lord spoke His word to Jonah, son of Amittai: "Get up, go to the great city of Nineveh and preach against it. I see the evil things they do."

But Jonah got up and ran away from the Lord. He went to the city of Joppa. There he found a ship that was going to the city of Tarshish. Jonah paid for the trip and went aboard. He wanted to go to Tarshish to run away from the Lord.

ACTIVITY TIME

Make a boat out of an old plastic bottle, some card and a small stick.

1 Draw round the bottle shape onto some card.

2 Fix card to bottle with string.

3 Pierce card and bottle and insert a stick with card taped to it. Write 'T' for Tarshish on the sail.

SPOT IN THE PICTURE

- ❖ Joppa
- ❖ Jonah
- ❖ The boat going to Tarshish
- ❖ The way to Nineveh

54

Jonah and His Fishy Tale

But the Lord sent a great wind on the sea. This wind made the sea very rough. So the ship was in danger of breaking apart. The sailors were afraid. Each man cried to his own god. The men began throwing the cargo into the sea. This would make the ship lighter so it would not sink.

But Jonah had gone down into the ship to lie down. He fell fast asleep.

CHECK IT OUT!
JONAH 1:1-5

QUIZ

1. Was Tarshish:
   a: on the way to Nineveh?
   b: in completely the opposite direction from Nineveh?

2. Was Nineveh:
   a: The capital of Assyria?
   b: The capital of France?

BRAINTEASER

Do some flower arranging. Find out what God told Jonah to do.

1✿ GET
4✿ TO
8✿ OF
13✿ IT
12✿ AGAINST
2✿ UP
10✿ AND
3✿ GO
9✿ NINEVEH
5✿ THE
7✿ CITY
6✿ GREAT
11✿ PREACH

Old Testament Activity Bible

Jonah Thrown Overboard

The men picked up Jonah and threw him into the sea.
JONAH 1:15

The captain of the ship came and said, "Why are you sleeping? Get up! Pray to your god! Perhaps your god will pay attention to us. Perhaps he will save us!"

The men said to Jonah, "Tell us what you have done. Why has this terrible thing happened to us? What is your job? Where do you come from? What is your country? Who are your people?"

Then Jonah said to them, "I am a Hebrew. I fear the Lord, the God of heaven. He is the God who made the sea and the land."

Then the men were very afraid. They asked Jonah,

BRAINTEASER

The word "and" comes five times in the story on these pages.

Match up the pairs of "ands," and write the words linked up by "and" together on a piece of paper.

The first part of the "and" pairs	The second part of the "and" pairs
PICK ME UP	SAID
JONAH	THROW
WIND	LAND
SEA	WAVES
CAME	THREW HIM

SPOT IN THE PICTURE

❖ Jonah
❖ The big fish
❖ waves

Jonah and His Fishy Tale

"What terrible thing did you do?" They knew Jonah was running away from the Lord because Jonah had told them.

The wind and the waves of the sea were becoming much stronger. So the men said to Jonah, "What should we do to you to make the sea calm down?"

Jonah said to them, "Pick me up, and throw me into the sea. Then it will calm down. I know it is my fault that this great storm has come on you."

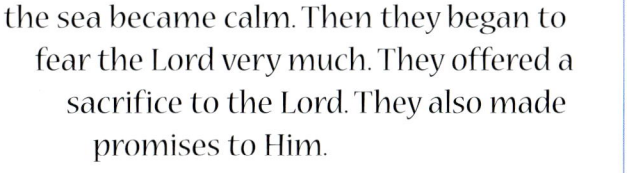

Then the men picked up Jonah and threw him into the sea. So the sea became calm. Then they began to fear the Lord very much. They offered a sacrifice to the Lord. They also made promises to Him.

CHECK IT OUT!
JONAH 1:6, 8-12, 15-16

U-N-J-U-M-B-L-E

Find out what happened when Jonah was thrown overboard.

Unjumble the words, and put them in the correct order.

M A C L

E H T

E M C E B A

E S A

WORD SEARCH

Make a list of the seven words hidden in this word search which come from the story on these pages. They are all written across or down.

G	S	A	F	R	A	I	D
X	E	Q	P	W	W	I	P
C	A	P	T	A	I	N	J
Z	F	E	Y	V	N	V	O
P	N	Y	M	E	D	V	N
O	V	C	Z	S	V	A	A
R	U	N	N	I	N	G	H

OLD TESTAMENT ACTIVITY BIBLE

JONAH IS RESCUED

And the Lord caused a very big fish to swallow Jonah. Jonah was in the stomach of the fish for three days and three nights. While Jonah was in the stomach of the fish, he prayed to the Lord his God. Jonah said,
"I was in danger.
So I called to the Lord,
and He answered me.

The Lord caused a very big fish to swallow Jonah.
JONAH 1:17

ACTIVITY TIME

Write out the text below. Then color in your letters to make it look really good.

"Salvation comes from the Lord!"

QUIZ

1. Jonah was rescued by:
   a: a boat
   b: a helicopter
   c: a fish

2. The type of fish that swallowed Jonah was:
   a: a whale
   b: a shark
   c: we are not told the type of fish

3. In the stomach of the very big fish Jonah:
   a: prayed
   b: watched satellite tv
   c: ate fish and chips

JONAH AND HIS FISHY TALE

I was about to die.
    So I cried to You,
      and You heard my voice.
You threw me into the sea.
    I went down, down into the deep sea.
The water was all around me.
    Your powerful waves flowed over me."
"Lord, I will praise and thank You
    while I give sacrifices to You.
I will make promises to You.
    And I will do what I promise.
Salvation comes from the Lord!"
Then the Lord spoke to the fish. And the fish spat Jonah out of its stomach onto the dry land.

CHECK IT OUT!
JONAH 1:17; 2:1-3, 9-10

CLOCKWORDS

In this puzzle there are two letters in place of each number on the clock face. To make a clockword, write down the letters of the hour hand mentioned, then the letters of the minute hand mentioned. So twenty to ten equals FI ND.

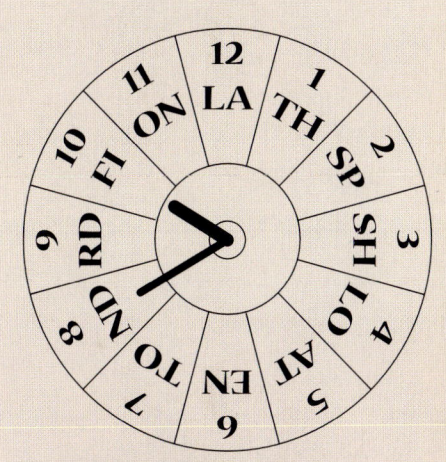

On a piece of paper fill in the blanks in the following sentence, using clockwords.

---- the ---- spoke to the ----. And the fish ---- Jonah out of its stomach ---- the dry ----.

a: Half past one
b: Quarter to four
c: Quarter past ten
d: Twenty five past two
e: Twenty five to eleven
f: Twenty to twelve

Jonah Preaches for God

Then the Lord spoke His word to Jonah again. The Lord said, "Get up. Go to the great city Nineveh. Preach against it what I tell you."

So Jonah obeyed the Lord. He got up and went to Nineveh. It was a very large city.

It took a person three days just to walk across it. Jonah entered the city. When he had walked for one day, he preached to the people. He said, "After 40 days, Nineveh will be destroyed!"

Jonah obeyed the Lord.
JONAH 3:3

BRAINTEASER

Write out each word as it should be spelled.

Put the words into the correct order.

IODNG
SUTM
YVEEERON
ARMH
POST

CORRECT

In the following sentence the only two correct words are "will be."

Put in the correct words.

"BEFORE 10 MONTHS, NEW YORK WILL BE HAPPY."

JONAH AND HIS FISHY TALE

The people of Nineveh believed in God. They announced that they would stop eating for a while. They put on rough cloth to show how sad they were. All the people in the city did this. People from the most important to the least important.

When the king of Nineveh heard this news, he got up from his throne. He took off his robe. He covered himself with rough cloth and sat in ashes to show how upset he was.

He made an announcement and sent it through the city…
People should cry loudly to God.
Everyone must turn away from his evil life.
Everyone must stop doing harm…

God saw what the people did. He saw that they had stopped doing evil things. So God changed His mind and did not do what He had warned. He did not punish them.

CHECK IT OUT!
JONAH 3:1-10

ACTIVITY TIME

BOOKMARK
Make a bookmark out of the words:

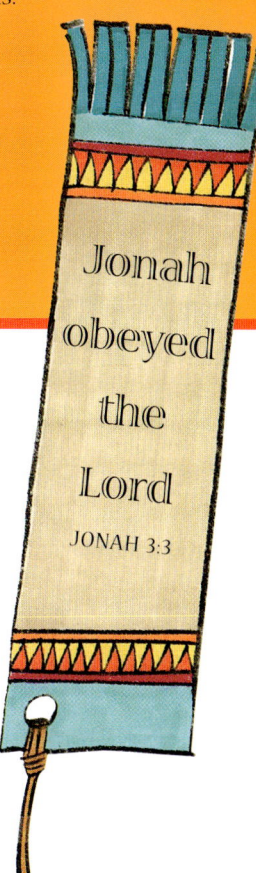

Jonah obeyed the Lord
JONAH 3:3

SPOT IN THE PICTURE
- Jonah
- The king of Nineveh
- The town of Nineveh

OLD TESTAMENT ACTIVITY BIBLE

ANSWERS

PAGES 4-5

FACT FILE
a: 450 feet (140 meters) long
b: 75 feet (23 meters) wide
c: 45 feet (13.5 meters) high
d: The ark was longer than today's planes.
Two points for each correct answer.

BRAINTEASER
c: 432 double decker buses could fit into the ark. Three points.

CHECK IT OUT!
Five points for reading this, or listening as it is read to you.

ACTIVITY TIME
Words linked to the story, like 'wood' and 'water' five points each.. Other words, one point each, up to a maximum of five words.

SPOT IN THE PICTURE
For any five from the following you score one point for each one you find, up to a maximum of five points: saw, nails, pincers, hammer, plank of wood, barrel of tar, brush for tar.
Record your total score for pages 4-5.

PAGES 6-7

MAKE A LIST
One point for each bird on your list.

A QUESTION ABOUT MR. NOAH
"Noah did everything that God commanded."
Three points.

MRS. NOAH
The four pairs of animals Mrs Noah has found are: Elephants, Giraffes, hippos (hippopotamuses), rhinos (rhinoceroses). One point for each pair you spotted.

CHECK IT OUT!
Five points for reading this, or listening as it is read to you.

WORD SEARCH
Ant, bee, beetle, flea, fly, moth, and spider. One point for each correct word.

SPOT IN THE PICTURE
The missing piles of fruit are apples, melons and grapes.
Two points for each pile of fruit you spotted.
Record your total score for pages 6-7.

PAGES 8-9

FIND THE MISSING
Two points for finding each pair of animals. Two more points if you remembered what they are called: Zebras and tigers.

ACTIVITY TIME
One point for each animal, bird, insect, or reptile.

FACT FILE
Seven. Three points.

CHECK IT OUT!
Five points for reading this, or listening as it is read to you.

QUIZ TIME
1c; 2b; 3a; 4b
Three points for each correct answer.
Record your total score for pages 8-9.

PAGES 10-11

ACTIVITY TIME
1. a: Shem; b: Ham; c: Japheth.
Two points for each son.
2. Their wives. Two points.

BRAINTEASER
Ham. Eight points.

CHECK IT OUT!
Five points for reading this, or listening as it is read to you.

FIND THE MISSING
Two points for finding each of Mrs. Noah's missing things: her comb, her coat, her belt.

FACT FILE
1c: The water covered the tops of the mountains by over 20 feet.
2c: Three points for each correct answer.

SPOT IN THE PICTURE
One point for finding animals, birds, insects, and reptiles.
Maximum of four points.
Record your total score for pages 10-11.

PAGES 12-13

DECODE
I am putting my rainbow in the clouds.
Two points for each correct word.

FACT FILE
a: The seven colors of the rainbow are: Violet, indigo, blue, green, yellow, orange, and red.
One point for each correct color.
b: The correct order of the colors of the rainbow are as listed above.
Five extra points if you put them in the correct order.
c: The color at the top of the rainbow is red. One point.
d: The color at the bottom of the rainbow is violet. One point.

CHECK IT OUT!
Five points for reading this, or listening as it is read to you.

DRAW YOUR OWN PICTURE
Five points for drawing a picture, plus one extra point for including each of the following: Noah's ark, the rainbow, a bird, an animal, and something that crawls on the earth.

WORD SEARCH
Rainbow, clouds, earth, boat, Noah, animals.
One point for each correct word.
Record your total score for pages 12-13.
Add up and record your total score from the story of Noah.

PAGES 14-15

ACTIVITY TIME
A word like "robe" linked to the story of Joseph scores two points. Other words, up to a maximum of five words score one point each.

QUIZ
a: 17 years old
b: Look after sheep
c: Joseph gave his father bad reports about his brothers.
d: Joseph was Jacob's favorite son.
Three points for each correct answer

CHECK IT OUT!
Five points for reading this, or listening as it is read to you.

BRAINTEASER
Israel loved Joseph more than his other sons.
Five points

SPOT IN THE PICTURE
One point for finding Jacob.
One point for each of Joseph's brothers, up to a maximum of eleven points.
Record your total score for pages 14-15.

PAGES 16-17

U-N-J-U-M-B-L-E
I saw the sun, moon and 11 stars bowing down to me.
Three points

DRAW
Five points for your drawing.
Five points for coloring or painting it.

SPOT IN THE PICTURE
One point for the sun.
One point for the moon.
One point for each star, to a maximum of eleven stars.

CHECK IT OUT!
Five points for reading this, or listening as it is read to you.

MATCH UP
11 bundles of wheat, bowing match with 11 brothers.
One bundle of wheat, not bowing matches with Joseph.
The sun matches with Jacob.
The moon matches with Joseph's mother.
11 stars, bowing match with 11 brothers.
Two points for each correct match you made.
Record your total score for pages 16-17.

PAGES 18-19

CLOCKWORDS
a: IN TO b: TH IS c: WE LL
d: HE RE
Three points for each correct word

CHECK IT OUT!
Five points for reading this, or listening as it is read to you.

UNSCRAMBLE
a: spices b: balm c: myrrh
Two points for each correct word

DECODE
Reuben planned to save Joseph later. Two points for each correct word.

SPOT IN THE PICTURE
One point for finding each of the things asked for.
Record your total score for pages 18-19.

PAGES 20-21

WORD SEARCH
Food, field, Potiphar, Egypt, servant, happy.
One point for each correct word.

CHECK IT OUT!
Five points for reading this, or listening as it is read to you.

QUIZ
a: Potiphar was captain of the palace guard - a top soldier.
b: The Lord blessed the people in Potiphar's house.
c: The Ishmaelites.
Three points for each correct answer.

UNRAVEL
The Lord was with Joseph.
Five points.

SPOT IN THE PICTURE
One point for finding each of the things asked for.
Record your total score for pages 20-21.

Answers

PAGES 22-23

ACTIVITY TIME
A word like "best" linked to the story of Joseph scores two points. Other words score one point.

RIGHT OR WRONG?
a: is wrong. b: is right.
Three points for each correct answer.

SPOT IN THE PICTURE
One point for seeing Joseph.
One point for seeing his six brothers.
One point for seeing Joseph's ring.
One point for seeing Joseph's fine linen clothes.
One point for seeing Joseph's gold chain.

CHECK IT OUT!
Five points for reading this, or listening as it is read to you.

SPOT THE WRONG THINGS
a: The king gave Joseph a ring from his own finger, fine linen clothes to wear and a gold chain.
b: Take some wagons from Egypt for their children and their wives.
One point for each word you corrected.

BRAINTEASER
Egypt, hugged, Benjamin, wagons, families, Canaan.
One point for each correct word.
Record your total score for pages 22-23.
Add up and record your total score from the story of Joseph.

PAGES 24-25

QUIZ TIME
a: Three months b: Reeds c: Tar d: Nile
Three points for each correct answer.

FACT FILE
1b; 2c; 3a
Three points for each correct answer.

CHECK IT OUT!
Five points for reading this, or listening as it is read to you.

ACTIVITY TIME
Five points for making a basket.
Five more points if it floats.

SPOT IN THE PICTURE
One point for finding each of the things asked for.
Record your total score for pages 24-25.

PAGES 26-27

WORD SEARCH
Milk, Mommy, rattle, crib, Daddy, smile.
One point for each correct answer.

THE KIND PRINCESS
a: Saw a baby boy
b: Felt sorry for him
c: Said, "This is one of the Hebrew babies."
Three points for each correct answer.

CHECK IT OUT!
Five points for reading this, or listening as it is read to you.

BRAINTEASER
a: to have a bath
Three points.

SPOT IN THE PICTURE
One point for finding each person asked for.
Record your total score for pages 26-27.

PAGES 28-29

DECODE
The king tried to kill Moses.
Two points for each correct word.

CHECK IT OUT!
Five points for reading this, or listening as it is read to you.

FACT FILE
c: Three points.

QUIZ
1c; 2a; 3a
Three points for each correct answer.
Record your total score for pages 28-29.

PAGES 30-31

BRAINTEASER
a: God heard their cries.
b: God saw the troubles his people suffered
.c: God was concerned about their pain.
d: God would bring them out of that land.
Three points for each correct answer.

ACTIVITY TIME
Five points for coloring in.

CHECK IT OUT!
Five points for reading this, or listening as it is read to you.

QUIZ TIME
a: It had lots of room.
d: There was much food.
Three points for each correct answer.

BACK TO FRONT
A land where much food grows.
Five points for putting in the correct order.
Record your total score for pages 30-31.

PAGES 32-33

REACH FOR YOUR CALCULATOR
If there were the same number of women as men = 600,000 women
If there were twice as many children as men = 1,200,000
men = 600,000
women = 600,000
children = 1,200,000
Total people = 2,400,000
a: = 2,400,000

If there were twice as many sheep as there were children = 2,400,000
If there were twice as many cattle as there were men = 1,200,000
If there were half as many goats as there were women = 300,000
Total number of animals leaving = 3,900,000
b: = 3,900,000

c: = 6,300,000
Three points for each correct answer. Double points if you did it without a calculator.

SPOT IN THE PICTURE
One point for each of the six things you found.

CHECK IT OUT!
Five points for reading this, or listening as it is read to you.

ACTIVITY
Five points for buying or baking unleavened bread.
Five points for tasting unleavened bread.

FIND THE MESSAGE
"Get up and leave my people." Two points for each correct word.

BRAINTEASER
c: 430 years Three points.
Record your total score for pages 32-33.

PAGES 34-35

ACTIVITY TIME
Ten points for making the book mark.

CHECK IT OUT!
Five points for reading this, or listening as it is read to you.

BRAINTEASER
1b; 2b; 3b

QUIZ TIME
a: Moses raised his staff, lifted it up.
b: Moses held his hand over the sea.
Three points for each correct answer.
Three points for each correct answer.
Record your total score for pages 34-35.
Add up and record your total score from the story of Moses.

PAGES 36-37

ACTIVITY TIME
Five points for weighing yourself or finding out or knowing your weight.
Five points for working out how many times heavier Goliath's scale armor was than your weight.

BRAINTEASER
Bronze, fighter, afraid, Saul, spear, helmet
One point for each correct answer.

CHECK IT OUT!
Five points for reading this, or listening as it is read to you.

SPOT IN THE PICTURE
One point for finding each of the things asked for.

FIND THE MESSAGE
"Today I stand and dare the army of Israel!"
One point for each correct word.
Record your total score for pages 36-37.

PAGES 38-39

QUIZ
a: Jesse
b: The commander
c: Early in the morning
Three points for each correct answer.

SPOT IN THE PICTURE
One point for finding each of the things asked for.

CHECK IT OUT!
Five points for reading this, or listening as it is read to you.

CLOCKWORDS
a: YO UR b: WI TH c: SA UL d: AR MY e: EL AH
Your brothers are with Saul and the army in the Valley of Elah.
Three points for each correct word.
Record your total score for pages 38-39.

PAGES 40-41

ACTIVITY TIME
Words linked to the story, like "line" five points each. Other words, one point each, up to a maximum of five words.

U-N-J-U-M-B-L-E
The king will give much money to the man who kills Goliath.
Five points

CHECK IT OUT!
Five points for reading this, or listening as it is read to you.

BRAINTEASER
When the Israelites saw Goliath, they were very much afraid and ran away.
Five points

SPOT IN THE PICTURE
One point for finding each of the things asked for.
Record your total score for pages 40-41.

63